TAYLOR · EDWARD JENNER · NABEEL
QURESHI · SIR ISAAC JIM
RWIN · JOHN HARPER · CHUCK COLSON
JIM ELLIOT · MARTIN LUTHER · ANDRÉ
TROCMÉ · HENRY OBOOKIAH · WILLIAM
BOOTH · ALVIN YORK · JOHN NEWTON
JUAN FERNANDO ORTEGA · WILLIAM
WILBERFORCE · RICHARD WURMBRAND
GEORGE MÜLLER · TONY DUNGY
G.K. CHESTERTON · TODD BEAMER
JAMES A. GARFIELD · JOHN M. PERKINS
SAINT FRANCIS OF ASSISI · ZHANG
BOLI · GEORGE WASHINGTON

ERIC LIDDEL · CHIUNE SUGIHARA
GEORGE WASHINGTON CARVER
DAVID LIVINGSTONE · NICKY CRUZ
TIM TEBOW · NATE SAINT · JESSE
BUSHYHEAD · WILLIAM TYNDALE
RICHARD ALLEN · FATHER DAMIEN
C.S. LEWIS · DIKEMBE MUTOMBO
JEREMY CAMP · ADONIRAM JUDSON
C. EVERETT KOOP · FRANCIS SCHAEFFER
JOHN CADBURY · BILLY GRAHAM
JEREMY LIN · JOHN KNOX · DON
MCCLANEN · DIETRICH BONHOEFFER
FREDERICK DOUGLASS · HUDSON

BRAVE HEROES AND BOLD DEFENDERS

by SHIRLEY RAYE REDMOND

ILLUSTRATIONS BY Katya Longhi

HARVEST HOUSE PUBLISHERS
EUGENE, OREGON

Scripture quotations are taken from the Holy Bible, New International Version®, NIV®. Copyright © 1973, 1978, 1984, 2011 by Biblica, Inc.® Used by permission. All rights reserved worldwide.

Published in association with Books & Such Literary Management, 52 Mission Circle, Suite 122, PMB 170, Santa Rosa, CA 95409-5370, www.booksandsuch.com.

Cover and interior illustrations by Katya Longhi

Cover design and hand lettering and interior design by Juicebox Designs

This logo is a federally registered trademark of The Hawkins Children's LLC. Harvest House Publishers, Inc., is the exclusive licensee of this trademark.

Brave Heroes and Bold Defenders

Text copyright © 2020 by Shirley Raye Redmond
Artwork copyright © 2020 by Harvest House Publishers

Published by Harvest House Publishers
Eugene, Oregon 97408
www.harvesthousepublishers.com

ISBN 978-0-7369-8133-0 (hardcover)

Library of Congress Cataloging-in-Publication Data is on file at the Library of Congress, Washington, DC.

All rights reserved. No part of this publication may be reproduced, stored in a retrieval system, or transmitted in any form or by any means—electronic, mechanical, digital, photocopy, recording, or any other—except for brief quotations in printed reviews, without the prior permission of the publisher.

Printed in Colombia

Contents

Introduction 7

Eric Liddell 8
Chiune Sugihara 10
George Washington Carver 12
David Livingstone 14
Nicky Cruz 16
Tim Tebow 18
Nate Saint 20
Jesse Bushyhead 22
William Tyndale 24
Richard Allen 26
Father Damien 28

C.S. Lewis 30
Dikembe Mutombo 32
Jeremy Camp 34
Adoniram Judson 36
C. Everett Koop 38
Francis Schaeffer 40
John Cadbury 42
Billy Graham 44
Jeremy Lin 46
John Knox 48
Don McClanen 50

Dietrich Bonhoeffer 52
Frederick Douglass 54
Hudson Taylor 56
Edward Jenner 58
Nabeel Qureshi 60
Sir Isaac Newton 62
Jim Irwin 64
John Harper 66
Chuck Colson 68
Jim Elliot 70
Martin Luther 72
André Trocmé 74
Henry Obookiah 76
William Booth 78

Alvin York 80
John Newton 82
Juan Fernando Ortega 84
William Wilberforce 86
Richard Wurmbrand 88
George Müller 90
Tony Dungy 92
G.K. Chesterton 94
Todd Beamer 96
James A. Garfield 98
John M. Perkins 100
Saint Francis of Assisi 102
Zhang Boli 104
George Washington 106

Notes 109

Introduction

In *The Abolition of Man*, C.S. Lewis lamented that the modern unchristian world no longer produces men of virtue, honor, integrity, and courage. He called faithless males "men without chests."

Fortunately, the men of faith profiled in this book do not fall into that category. Brave, smart, and sometimes unconventional, they changed the world for the better, looking to Jesus as their role model. They did not allow fear or anxiety to limit their dedication to serving Christ. They often struggled to bring his truth and light into a world of darkness—sometimes at great risk to themselves and their families.

From inventors and physicians to missionaries and athletes, these courageous men dedicated their lives to serving the Lord. Like Jesus, some were reviled and mocked. Others faced life-threatening circumstances with great courage. A few paid the ultimate price—dying for the gospel. They are all heroes of the Christian faith.

Their lives will inspire and challenge you to live out your own faith in bold and innovative ways, to "shine...like stars in the sky as you hold firmly to the word of life" (Philippians 2:15-16). These are men of true grit.

Eric Liddell

Gold Medal Runner

{ 1902–1945 }

Quiet and shy, Eric Liddell loved math, chemistry, and sports. At age sixteen, he astonished everyone at his Scottish boarding school when he took first place in three track and field events.

Eric was born in China to Scottish missionaries. He grew up loving the Lord. When he entered the University of Edinburgh, he joined the track team, earning the nickname the Flying Scotsman because of his speed. As his fame grew, Eric had opportunities to address large crowds. He always mentioned his faith in Christ.

At age twenty-two, Eric earned a place on the British Olympic Team to compete in the 100-meter race at the 1924 Paris games. However, when he learned the race would take place on Sunday—the Lord's Day—he refused to run. His decision angered the Olympic committee. When Eric offered to run the 400-meter race on Monday, few expected him to win.

Eric thrilled his fans by winning the gold medal and setting a new world record. His stunning victory is portrayed in the Academy Award–winning film *Chariots of Fire*. Eric returned to China as a missionary, met his wife, Florence, and had three daughters.

In 1937, Japan declared war on China. Eric moved his family to Canada and then returned alone to China. Captured by the Japanese, Eric joyfully ministered to his fellow prisoners. When selected to participate in a prisoner exchange, Eric allowed a pregnant woman to take his place. He died from a brain tumor five months before the Allies liberated the camp. The world mourned him.

ERIC LIDDELL

Chiune Sugihara
Holocaust Hero

{ 1900–1986 }

Chiune Sugihara was born in Japan. His father, a physician, wanted Chiune to follow in his footsteps. Chiune had other plans. At age nineteen, he received a Foreign Ministry scholarship and traveled to China to learn Russian and German. During this time, he was baptized into the Russian Orthodox Church.

In 1939, Chiune and his wife, Yukiko, moved to the capital of Lithuania to take up his post as vice consul at the Japanese embassy. They had barely settled in when the Nazi army invaded Poland. This resulted in a flood of desperate Jewish refugees streaming from Poland into Lithuania.

Word quickly spread about the holocaust—the organized killing of Jews ordered by Adolf Hitler. Sugihara signed thousands of exit visas permitting Jewish refugees to flee to Japan, even though Tokyo officials had forbidden him to do so. Sugihara told his wife, "I may have to disobey my government, but if I do not, I will be disobeying God."[1]

Frantic Jewish refugees climbed over the wall of the Japanese embassy in Lithuania, hoping to secure exit visas from the compassionate Sugihara. Risking disgrace and dismissal, he continued to sign visas to help more Jews escape the deadly holocaust. When suddenly ordered to return to Japan, Sugihara threw signed exit visas out of the train window to refugees.

Forced to resign from the civil service, Sugihara supported his family by performing menial tasks and selling lightbulbs door-to-door. After the war, the grateful state of Israel honored Chiune Sugihara and his wife by declaring them "Righteous Among the Nations."

George Washington Carver
Agricultural Visionary

{ 1864–1943 }

When George Washington Carver was a baby, he and his mother were kidnapped by slave raiders. German immigrants Moses and Susan Carver rescued George, who never saw his mother again. Mrs. Carver taught George to read the Bible, and he did so every day for the rest of his life.

In high school, George loved botany, chemistry, and art. He applied to a Kansas college and was accepted, but the dean withdrew the acceptance after discovering George was African American. At age thirty, George applied to Iowa State College to study horticulture. He was accepted, but he was banned from the student cafeteria and forced to eat in the kitchen.

When George graduated with a master's degree in 1896, Booker T. Washington invited him to teach at the Tuskegee Institute in Alabama. With no laboratory funding, George scoured junkyards to find broken bottles to use as beakers. He used ink bottles and string for Bunsen burners. He experimented with peanuts and sweet potatoes, discovering hundreds of uses for them. He gained national recognition for his syndicated newspaper column about agricultural topics, such as crop rotation. During World War II, he intrigued inventor Henry Ford by producing artificial rubber from milkweed.

Carver donated his life savings to a research institute at Tuskegee. He always credited God for his success. In a letter to friends, he wrote, "Oh how I wish the people would awake from their lethargy and come out body and soul for Christ."[2]

Carver was inducted into the National Inventors Hall of Fame in 1990.

George Washington Carver

David Livingstone

God's Trailblazer

{ 1813–1872 }

David Livingstone was born in Scotland. He worked in cotton mills, propping books against the machinery so he could read. He studied theology and medicine and longed to be a missionary to China, but international politics prevented him from going there. In 1840, he sailed for Africa. He married missionary Robert Moffat's daughter, Mary.

David wrote reports about the appalling Arab slave trade. He explored rivers and jungles. Once a lion attacked him, crushing his right arm. He justified the risks, saying, "But who that believes in Jesus would refuse to make a venture for such a Captain?"[3]

In 1856, he returned to England with his family. He was now a national hero, and his books became bestsellers. But the London Missionary Society claimed his explorations distracted Livingstone from his duties as a missionary, so he resigned.

David returned to Africa to map the Zambezi River. He named Victoria Falls for the Queen. On his journeys, Livingstone took an early version of a slide projector to show scenes depicting Bible stories to the natives.

When two years passed without any word from Livingstone, the *New York Herald* sent reporter Henry Stanley to find him, which he did in 1869. Livingstone led Stanley to Christ but refused to leave Africa. One morning, native servants found Livingstone dead, kneeling by his cot. They buried his heart beneath a tree, and his remains were shipped back to England.

God used David Livingstone to focus attention on conditions in Africa and to inspire generations of missionaries to serve there.

Nicky Cruz
God's Gangster

{ 1938–PRESENT }

One of nineteen children, Nicky Cruz was born in a poverty-stricken neighborhood in Puerto Rico. His parents practiced witchcraft and cruelly abused him. Nicky tried to commit suicide when he was nine. When he turned fifteen, his father sent Nicky to New York City to live with relatives. There, Nicky joined a terrible gang known as the Mau Maus and soon became the gang leader. His life was filled with violence and substance abuse. He suffered from nightmares, which grew worse after his best friend died in his arms from stab wounds.

Pastor David Wilkerson tried to convince Nicky that Christ loved him. Enraged, Nicky slapped him. Wilkerson never gave up, pursuing him with relentless love. Months later, during an evangelistic rally at a boxing arena, Nicky surrendered his life to Jesus. Other gang members did too. They stunned police by turning in their handguns and knives.

Nicky attended Bible college to become a pastor, and then he returned to his New York neighborhood to preach. He married and had four children. His conversion story is told in Wilkerson's bestselling book *The Cross and the Switchblade*, which later became a movie starring Erik Estrada and Pat Boone.

Nicky's autobiography, *Run Baby Run*, has sold millions of copies and is required reading in many European urban schools. Through Nicky Cruz Outreach, an evangelistic organization, Nicky has preached the gospel all over the world.

NICKY✝CRUZ

Tim Tebow

Faithful Football Athlete

{ 1987–PRESENT }

The first time Tim Tebow dropped to one knee, resting his head on his hand to pray, he started a cultural trend. Fans imitated him. Others mocked him. The gesture became known as "Tebowing."

The youngest of five children, Tim was born in the Philippines to American missionaries. He was homeschooled by his mother, and his Christian faith has always been an important part of his life. In 2006, Tim won a football scholarship to play for the University of Florida Gators. He gained notoriety by wearing Bible verses in his eye black. He won the Heisman Trophy in 2007 for his skill on the field and led his team to win the Bowl Championship Series twice. When the NFL Broncos drafted Tim, he measured six feet three and weighed 240 pounds. He is said to be one of the strongest men to ever play quarterback. He later joined the New York Jets in 2012. Despite some negative media attention during his sports career, Tebow remained unflinching in his faith. He is now a professional baseball player and broadcaster.

Tebow founded the Tim Tebow Foundation in January 2010, a faith-based organization that builds playrooms in hospitals and grants wishes for children with life-threatening diseases. In 2018, he and his brother served as executive producers for the inspirational sports movie *Run the Race*. He has written several books, including *This Is the Day*, encouraging others to find their purpose in Christ.

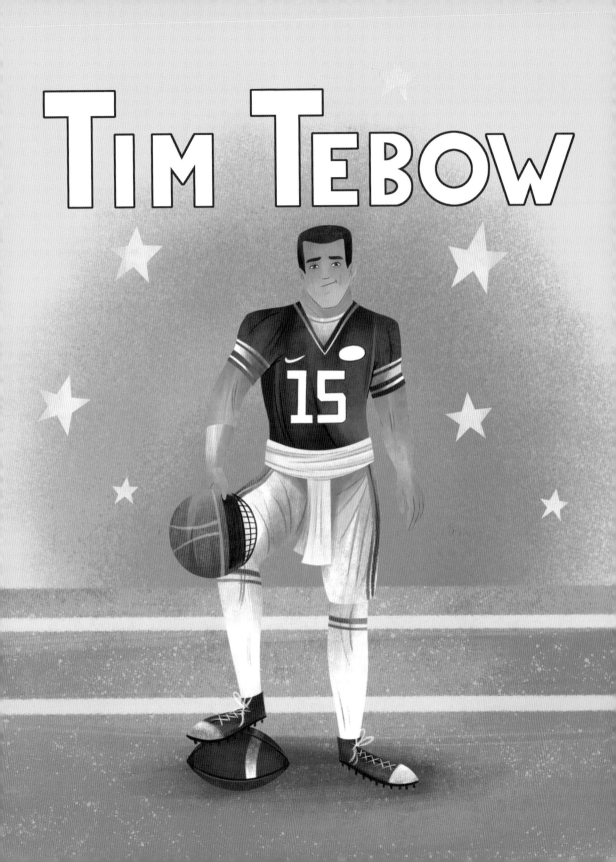

Nate Saint

Missionary Pilot

{ 1923–1956 }

Nate Saint jokingly referred to himsef as a grease monkey for the Lord. He grew up in a family committed to Christian missions. Nate enjoyed his first airplane flight at age seven and took flying lessons in high school. During World War II, he joined the Army Air Corps. But because of a leg infection, Nate was declared unfit for military flying when he was nineteen.

After the war, Nate joined the Missionary Aviation Fellowship (MAF). His first task was to salvage a crashed MAF airplane. Nate used his mechanical ingenuity to repair the plane and fly it out of a Mexican jungle.

After attending Wheaton College, Nate married Marjorie Ferris in 1948, and they moved to Ecuador. Nate invented many gadgets used by missionary pilots today, including the dual-injection engine and the bucket drop. He used this technique to deliver gifts to the Waorani tribe, hoping to make friendly contact. Called Aucas (or savages) by other natives, the Waorani were feared because of their frequent killing sprees.

Encouraged by the exchange of gifts, Nate and four other missionaries camped beside a river near the Waorani village. Nate even took one of the villagers for an airplane ride. But the friendliness did not last. The Waorani killed the missionaries with spears.

Nate did not die in vain. The tribe was eventually evangelized by Rachel Saint (Nate's sister) and Elisabeth Elliot, the wife of Jim Elliot, one of the other missionaries who had been killed. Two of Nate's children were later baptized by one of the converted warriors who had killed their father.

Jesse Bushyhead

Cherokee Preacher

{ 1804–1844 }

Born in a small Cherokee settlement in Tennessee, Jesse Bushyhead was educated at the Candy Creek mission school. His Cherokee name was Unadati. He accepted Christ at age twenty-six and was later ordained as a Baptist minister. He served as an interpreter for Reverend Evan Jones, a missionary from Wales who ministered among the Cherokees for more than fifty years.

Tragedy struck from 1836 through 1839, when President Andrew Jackson, followed by President Martin Van Buren, forced the Cherokees to give up their farms and homes to the United States government. The Cherokees were ordered to move west to Oklahoma Territory. Bushyhead and Jones protested this unfair treatment but were unable to negotiate a peaceful resolution.

Month after month, large groups of disheartened Cherokees headed west on the Trail of Tears. Soldiers ensured their departure remained orderly. In 1838, Bushyhead reluctantly began leading a party of approximately 1,000 Cherokee men, women, and children on a trip that would span more than 1,200 miles. Many people died along the way from cholera, whooping cough, and other diseases. Food was scarce too. Throughout the long journey, Bushyhead continued to preach, encouraging the people to place their hope in Jesus Christ.

On their arrival in 1839, near present-day Westville, Oklahoma, Bushyhead established a Baptist mission. He became chief justice of the Cherokee nation in 1840 and served in that office until he died from a brief illness at age forty. His grave marker notes that Bushyhead "died as he lived, a devoted Christian."

JESSE BUSHYHEAD

William Tyndale

Bold Bible Translator

{ 1494–1536 }

If you have an English language Bible in your home, you can thank courageous William Tyndale.

William grew up on a farm in England. Because he was bright and had a flair for languages, his parents sent him to Oxford to study theology when he was twelve years old. There he learned seven languages, including Hebrew, Greek, and Latin. In those days, most Englishmen didn't own Bibles. At church services, the Scriptures were read in Latin—a language only well-educated people understood. Tyndale believed God wanted him to give his countrymen a Bible they could read on their own, but doing so was against the law.

In 1524, Tyndale sailed across the English Channel to Europe. He would never see his homeland or family again. In Germany, he worked secretly to translate the New Testament into English. A sympathetic printer produced 6,000 copies, which were smuggled into England, sometimes hidden at the bottom of flour barrels. The books sold quickly.

The King of England and church officials declared Tyndale an outlaw and sent spies to find him. Betrayed by a friend, Tyndale was arrested and imprisoned in a castle dungeon. He was eventually hanged, and his body was burned. Tyndale's last words were, "Lord, please open the King of England's eyes."[4]

Not long afterward, King Henry VIII saw a copy of Tyndale's New Testament and permitted English language Bibles to be printed and sold throughout England. God had answered Tyndale's final prayer.

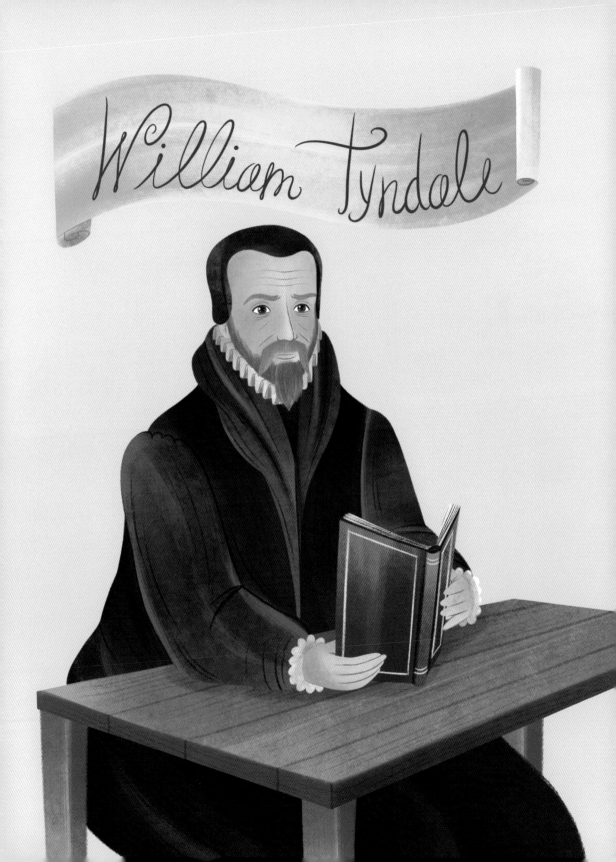

Richard Allen

Megachurch Minister

{ 1760–1831 }

Richard Allen grew up as a slave on a Delaware plantation. He taught himself to read and write. No one imagined he would become a famous preacher and the founder of the African Methodist Episcopal Church (AME).

At age seventeen, Richard attended a revival at a nearby Methodist church. He accepted Christ as his Savior and began preaching on the plantation. One of his earliest converts was his owner, Stokely Sturgis, who was so impressed with Richard's abilities that he allowed him to work for others to earn enough money to buy his freedom. Sturgis eventually allowed other slaves to do the same. Richard became a circuit rider, preaching at Methodist churches in Delaware and surrounding states. Prominent white church leaders were impressed. In Philadelphia, he attended Saint George's Methodist Church. His leadership at prayer meetings soon attracted many African Americans, but racial tensions increased when they were told to sit along the walls, not in the pews.

Incidents like this prompted Richard to open his own church, where African Americans could worship with dignity. Together with his friend Absalom Jones, Richard bought a blacksmith's building and opened the doors to the first AME church.

Richard's first wife died from illness. He had six children with his second wife, Sarah, who helped operate a station on the Underground Railroad for escaping slaves. Together, Richard and Sarah oversaw the rapid growth of their congregation to an incredible 7,500 people in the 1820s. Today, AME congregations are located in thirty-nine countries on five continents.

RICHARD ALLEN

Father Damien

Loving the Lepers

Joseph de Veuster was born on a farm in Belgium and raised by devout Catholic parents. Longing to be a missionary, Joseph entered the priesthood, adopting the name Damien. In 1863, he sailed to Honolulu in the kingdom of Hawaii. There he heard about the plight of seven hundred incurable lepers—some of them children—banished by the king to the island of Molokai.

Leprosy, or Hansen's disease, results in seeping skin lesions and a loss of feeling. Touched with compassion, Damien moved to Molokai, grimly referred to as the island of the living dead. With the help of his patients, he tore down shacks and constructed comfortable huts. He established farms and organized schools. He built a church and formed a children's choir. He changed bandages and dug graves.

Inspired by Damien's bold leadership and hearty laugh, the community thrived. News of his success rippled through Hawaii and around the world. Money poured in to support his labor of love. Protestant churches joined in sending clothing, food, and other supplies.

For more than ten years, Damien served the isolated community. Then one day, while washing his feet, he could not feel the hot water. Damien realized he had contracted the dreaded disease. He served until bedridden. In one of his last letters he wrote, "My face and my hands are already decomposing, but the good Lord is calling me to keep Easter with Himself."[5]

Damien died at age forty-nine. He was canonized in 2009, becoming Hawaii's first saint.

FATHER DAMIEN

C.S. Lewis
Creator of Narnia

{ 1898–1963 }

Clive Staples Lewis grew up in Ireland. He and his brother, Warren, enjoyed creating stories about talking animals and noble knights. Jack, as he liked to be called, lost his mother to cancer when he was ten. Angry and grieving, Jack turned his back on God. At nineteen, he joined the British army to fight in France during World War I. Wounded by shrapnel, he was sent home the following year. After graduating from Oxford University, Lewis accepted a teaching position there. He joined a group of writers called the Inklings. Conversations with J.R.R. Tolkien and other members led Lewis to accept Christ in 1929.

During World War II, he gave a series of popular radio broadcasts about Christianity. These speeches were published in the book *Mere Christianity*. He opened his home to schoolgirls evacuated from war-torn London. The experience inspired his children's book *The Lion, the Witch and the Wardrobe*—the first title in the Chronicles of Narnia series. After the war, Prime Minister Winston Churchill notified Lewis that he wished to bestow upon him an honorary title. Lewis politely declined to avoid being associated with any political issues.

Besides writing books, Lewis personally answered thousands of letters from fans around the world. In 1954, he joined the literature faculty of Cambridge University. At age fifty-eight, he married Joy Gresham, a divorced American woman with whom he had corresponded for several years.

Lewis died on November 22, 1963—the same day President John F. Kennedy was assassinated. Few dispute that C.S. Lewis is the most widely read and most often quoted Christian author of the modern age.

C. S. Lewis

Dikembe Mutombo
NBA Legend

{ 1966–PRESENT }

One of ten children, Dikembe Mutombo was born in the Democratic Republic of the Congo. He grew up in a devout Christian family. His parents taught him the importance of education, faith, and charity. Dikembe says, "We were accustomed to having strangers in the house because my mother never turned away anyone who was hungry or needed a safe place to sleep."[6]

Deke came to the United States in 1987 to attend Georgetown University in Washington, DC, on an academic scholarship. When the basketball coach noticed the new student was seven feet, two inches tall, he suggested Deke try out for the basketball team. Deke quickly made a name for himself on the court.

Immediately after graduating in 1991 with degrees in diplomacy and linguistics, Deke was drafted by the Denver Nuggets of the National Basketball Association (NBA). Deke earned a reputation as one of the greatest shot blockers and defensive players of all time, leading the NBA in blocked shots for five consecutive seasons and most blocks per game for a record-breaking three consecutive seasons. After retiring from the Houston Rockets in 2009, Mutombo became the first Global Ambassador for the NBA, traveling throughout Africa, Asia, and the Middle East promoting various NBA programs, such as Basketball Without Borders.

Mutombo was honored with the 2019 Atlanta Sports Council's Lifetime Achievement Award, presented by Coca-Cola. As president of the Dikembe Mutombo Foundation, he works to improve health and education for the citizens of the Congo. The Biamba Marie Mutombo Hospital, named in honor of his mother, has treated more than 100,000 women and children.

Dikembe Mutombo

Jeremy Camp
Steadfast Singer

{ 1978–PRESENT }

B orn and raised in Indiana, the son of a pastor, Jeremy Camp showed a keen interest in music from an early age. He learned to play guitar from his father. After high school, Jeremy attended Calvary Chapel Bible College in California. The school's worship leader heard Jeremy performing in the dormitory and encouraged him to join the school's music ministry program.

Soon Jeremy began playing at Christian music events throughout California. He released his CD *Burden Me* in 2000. He married Melissa Henning that same year. Sadly, she died from ovarian cancer in 2001. Heartbroken, Jeremy poured out his sorrow and undiminished faith in Jesus through his music. Songs such as "I Still Believe" earned him a reputation as a talented Christian musician.

In 2002, Jeremy signed with BEC Recordings, who distributed his album *Stay* to a national audience. Five of the songs reached the top of the Christian singles charts. Jeremy married singer Adrienne Liesching in 2003, and they now have three children. With a renewed heart for evangelism, Jeremy wanted to take the message of Christ into the world through his music and practical service. Following the success of his album *Speaking Louder Than Before*, Jeremy and his wife established Speaking Louder, a nonprofit organization, in 2012. The Camps help Syrian and Iraqi refugees to find homes and jobs.

The multi-award-winning vocalist has shared his music in thirty-six countries. He continues to give testimony of his faith through his songs and his popular memoir, *I Still Believe*.

Adoniram Judson
Celebrity Missionary

{ 1788–1850 }

P rison chains, tropical fevers, rats, and fleas—Adoniram Judson endured them all for the sake of Christ.

Born in Massachusetts, Adoniram was a preacher's kid and a bookworm. He began reading Bible verses at age three. He graduated at the top in his class at Brown University at nineteen. During this time, he rejected his faith, influenced by a disbelieving friend. Determined to become a playwright, Adoniram journeyed to New York City. Failure and the unexpected death of his friend forced Adoniram to return home. He recommitted his life to Christ, enrolled in Andover Theological Seminary, and became interested in missions.

In 1812, Judson and his wife, Ann Hasseltine, sailed for Asia as part of the first American foreign missionary team. They endured many hardships in Burma, including a harsh climate, disease, and the death of a child. Suspected of being a spy, Judson was imprisoned. Through Ann's prayers and the intervention of the British military, Judson was released.

But the hardships continued. He buried Ann, his second wife Sarah, and several children. Depressed and grieving, Judson worked on his Burmese Bible translation. When he returned to America after a thirty-three-year absence, he discovered he was a national celebrity. Thousands attended his lectures. Donations poured in for missions. In 1846, Judson married Eliza Chubbock and returned to Burma. Although he soon died from a lung infection, his work proved fruitful. He had completed his Bible translation and produced a Burmese-English dictionary. He helped establish sixty-three churches with native pastors and thousands of converts. Burma—now called Myanmar—has millions of Christians today.

ADONIRAM JUDSON

C. Everett Koop

Pediatrics Pioneer

{ 1916–2013 }

Born in Brooklyn, the only child of a banker, Charles Koop was only six when he decided to become a surgeon. He developed his dexterity by cutting out magazine pictures. He learned to tie knots with one hand. As a teenager, Charles volunteered at the local hospital. He performed a leg operation under a doctor's supervision when he was only nineteen.

Charles attended Dartmouth College on a football scholarship. There he earned the nickname Chick. He gave up football after an eye injury. In medical school, he married Betty Flanagan, and the couple had four children. Specializing in pediatric surgery, Koop invented a device to prevent anesthesia overdoses in babies. He developed procedures to correct common birth defects in newborns. He gained international fame by successfully separating conjoined twins.

Koop championed the rights of the unborn and the physically impaired. In 1979, he collaborated with theologian Francis Schaeffer to produce the film series Whatever Happened to the Human Race? When nominated for the position of US Surgeon General during Ronald Reagan's presidency, Koop met with fierce opposition because of his Christian activism. Opponents called him Dr. Kook. Undaunted, Koop said, "I felt the Lord's assurance when I needed it the most."[7]

As surgeon general, he educated the public about tobacco use and secondhand smoke. He warned about health issues related to pornography. He was the first federal authority to publish a report on acquired immune deficiency syndrome (AIDS). After resigning, Koop continued to write and lecture on health care. His surgical innovations are still used today.

C. Everett Koop

Francis Schaeffer

Intellectual Giant

{ 1912–1984 }

Francis Schaeffer is considered a Christian intellectual giant of the twentieth century. His was a household name in evangelical circles from the 1960s through the 1980s. But Fran, as his friends called him, wasn't always Christ's champion. As a youth, Fran doubted that God existed. At Hampden-Sydney College, he read the Bible, and it changed his life.

He met Edith Seville at a lecture, where they both publicly disagreed with the speaker's ungodly views. They married in 1935. Edith encouraged Fran to attend seminary. In 1948, the Schaeffers and their four youngsters traveled to Switzerland as missionaries. There, Schaeffer founded the L'Abri Fellowship in 1955. He welcomed hippies, drug addicts, dropouts, and disillusioned Christians. Dressed in knickers and knee socks, Schaeffer taught them about Christ in ways no one had ever taught them before. He tackled issues such as pollution and racism from a Christian worldview.

Sometimes struggling with depression, Schaeffer found time to write twenty-two thought-provoking and influential books. In 1979, his bestselling book *Whatever Happened to the Human Race?*, written with C. Everett Koop, ignited pro-life activism. He wrote *A Christian Manifesto* in 1981 in response to *The Communist Manifesto*, a pamphlet written by Karl Marx and Friedrich Engels in 1848.

Schaeffer said, "One of the greatest injustices we do to our young people is to ask them to be conservative. Christianity is not conservative, but revolutionary."[8] The Francis A. Schaeffer Foundation and the L'Abri Fellowship, with branches in Switzerland, South Korea, and the United States, are active tributes to his life's work.

Francis Schaeffer

John Cadbury

Chocolate Bar Benefactor

{ 1801–1889 }

One of ten children, John Cadbury was born into a religious Quaker family in England. As he teenager, he worked for a tea merchant. Later, he opened his own shop, selling tea, coffee, and chocolate drinks. He hoped these would be healthy alternatives to alcoholic beverages. As his business prospered, John built a factory and hired thousands of employees. He made chocolates and designed decorative boxes to sell them in.

John believed alcohol consumption caused poverty, violence, and health problems. He also disapproved of war and slavery. He raised his sons, George and Richard, to take their faith seriously. He encouraged Bible reading and prayer at the factory each morning. The Cadburys became famous for their generous treatment of their workers. They paid good wages and gave weekends off. Other businessmen soon followed their example.

John campaigned against child labor and started a society to prevent cruelty to animals. In 1854, he received his first Royal Warrant from Queen Victoria. Cadbury chocolates became the official choice of the Queen of England!

Following the death of his wife in 1855, John's health failed. He turned the business over to George and Richard. The Cadburys moved their factory out of the crowded city and built a village with bright homes, gardens, and sports facilities for their employees. They even created new kinds of treats, like cream-filled Easter eggs.

Today Cadbury is one of the largest confectionery companies in the world.

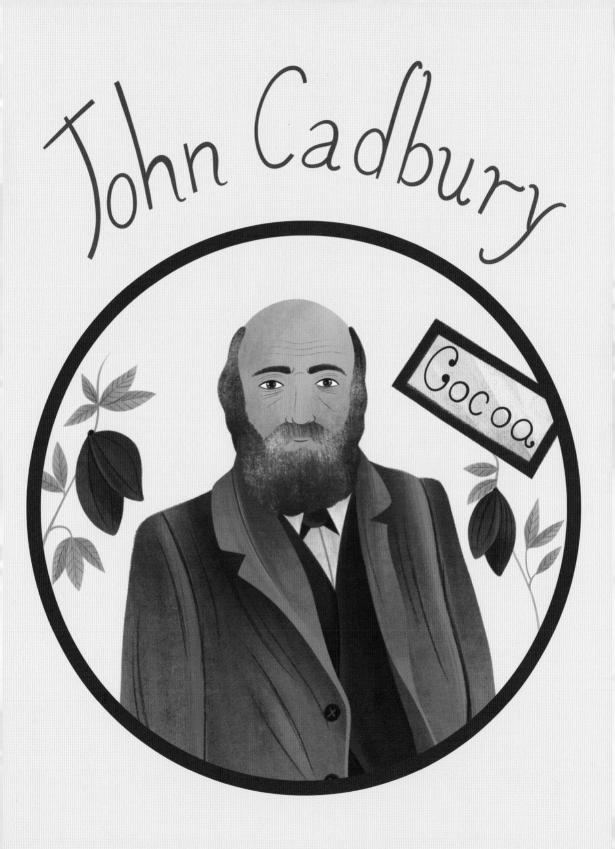

Billy Graham
Superstar Evangelist

{ 1918-2018 }

Billy Graham grew up on a dairy farm in North Carolina. The eldest of four children, he followed the moral values of his Christian parents. While still a teenager, Billy attended a revival led by evangelist Mordecai Ham. Billy later wrote, "I did not know Jesus for myself. I could not depend on my parents' faith."[9] He took his new commitment seriously, becoming an ordained Baptist minister at age twenty-one. He married Ruth Bell, and together they raised five children. Billy preached at revivals and crusades. In a world fearful of the destructive power of nuclear weapons, Billy offered hope in Jesus.

Billy achieved nationwide fame when several celebrities, including Roy Rogers and Dale Evans, were converted at the 1949 Los Angeles crusade. He boldly spoke out on race relations, proclaiming that God's love knows no racial barriers. In 1952, while preaching in Tennessee, he personally removed the ropes separating the blacks from the whites.

Some British politicians demanded a boycott of Graham's 1954 London crusade because of his antisocialist and anticommunist remarks. Billy and his staff prayed that God would be glorified. That night the arena, which seated 22,000 people, was filled to overflowing. Graham stayed for three months, preaching to ever-growing audiences.

Featured on the cover of *Time* magazine in 1954, Graham became the most famous evangelist in the world. He is credited with preaching the gospel to more people than anyone in history, reaching 200 million people in 185 countries through radio, television, and the written word.

BILLY GRAHAM

Jeremy Lin
Basketball Marvel

{ 1988–PRESENT }

Jeremy Lin loved basketball from the moment his father taught him and his two brothers how to play.

Born in California to Taiwanese immigrants, Jeremy grew up in a loving Christian home. In high school, he began to take his faith seriously. He also became serious about basketball, leading his school team to the California Interscholastic Federation Division II state title his senior year. He was also named the Northern California Division II Player of the Year. Despite his spectacular athletic ability, he did not receive a basketball scholarship.

At Harvard, Jeremy earned an economics degree and played basketball. He became a finalist for both the John R. Wooden Award for outstanding college player of the year and the Bob Cousy Award for top point guard. Jeremy hoped to be drafted by the National Basketball Association (NBA) in 2010, but he wasn't. Things changed when the New York Knicks signed him for the 2011–2012 season. Jeremy's court performance played a key role in the team's amazing winning streak. Scoring more points in his first five NBA starts than any other player in modern history, Jeremy sparked a global frenzy dubbed Linsanity. He made *Time* magazine's list of the one hundred most influential people in the world.

Jeremy has faced illness and injuries that sometimes prevented him from playing. He has also coped with discrimination in a sport dominated by African Americans.

Today Jeremy continues to travel and play professional basketball. On the road he listens to taped sermons, saying, "When you think about your relationship with Christ, it really just affects every aspect of your life."[10]

Jeremy Lin

John Knox

Revolutionary Reformer

{ 1514–1572 }

John Knox incited riots. He angered monarchs. But his vigorous sermons enthralled thousands, igniting a spiritual revolution in Scotland.

The son of a humble farmer, John studied theology at the University of St Andrews and became a Catholic priest in 1536. At this time, the Roman Catholic Church owned more than half the land in Scotland, bringing in eighteen times more revenue than the Scottish king.

Despite the dangers, Knox embraced Protestantism in 1542. Carrying a double-edged sword, he became a bodyguard for Scottish reformer George Wishart. After Wishart was executed as a heretic, an outraged Knox served as garrison chaplain at St Andrews Castle. In 1547, the French attacked the castle, taking everyone captive, including Knox, who was forced into slave labor aboard a galley ship. He spent nineteen months chained to an oar.

Freed in 1549, Knox became chaplain to Edward VI, the Protestant King of England. When Edward died, his sister Queen Mary ordered the execution of Protestant clergymen. Knox fled to Europe, where he became friends with theologian John Calvin. Knox married twice and had five children. Risking death, Knox returned to Scotland, where he established the Presbyterian Church. A would-be assassin fired a shot through the window where Knox often sat with his back to the street. The bullet passed through the chair, shattering a chandelier. Knox, sitting in a different chair, remained unharmed.

Knox's influence has spread far and wide. For example, today there are twice as many Presbyterians in Korea than in Scotland, and many Korean Christians visit Knox's homeland.

John Knox

Don McClanen
Valiant Coach

{ 1925–2016 }

Don McClanen had a dream. If professional athletes were willing to endorse cereal, shaving cream, and other products, could he convince Christian athletes to boldly promote Jesus Christ?

Born in Trenton, New Jersey, McClanen always loved sports. After serving in the Navy during World War II, he earned a college degree at Oklahoma State University. He and his wife, Gloria, had four children. He coached high school basketball and went on to become the men's basketball coach at Eastern Oklahoma University.

McClanen noticed the hero status enjoyed by popular sports figures. Learning that 30 million youngsters in the United States had no spiritual training, he wondered if he could influence them through sports. He cut out newspaper articles about Christian athletes and posted them in locker rooms. He prayed before games. He dreamed of a world transformed by Jesus Christ through the influence of dedicated Christian coaches and athletes.

McClanen asked nineteen well-known Christian athletes to help establish an organization that would encourage others to speak out boldly for Jesus. Fourteen of them eagerly agreed. McClanen joined forces with other coaches and Christian businessmen to charter the Fellowship of Christian Athletes (FCA) in 1954. His dream had become a movement.

Today the FCA continues to encourage coaches and athletes to dedicate their sports careers to Christ. McClanen's legacy has had a far-reaching effect through 14,000 campus huddles in eighty-four countries. More than 88,000 youngsters attend FCA sports camps each year.

Don McClanen

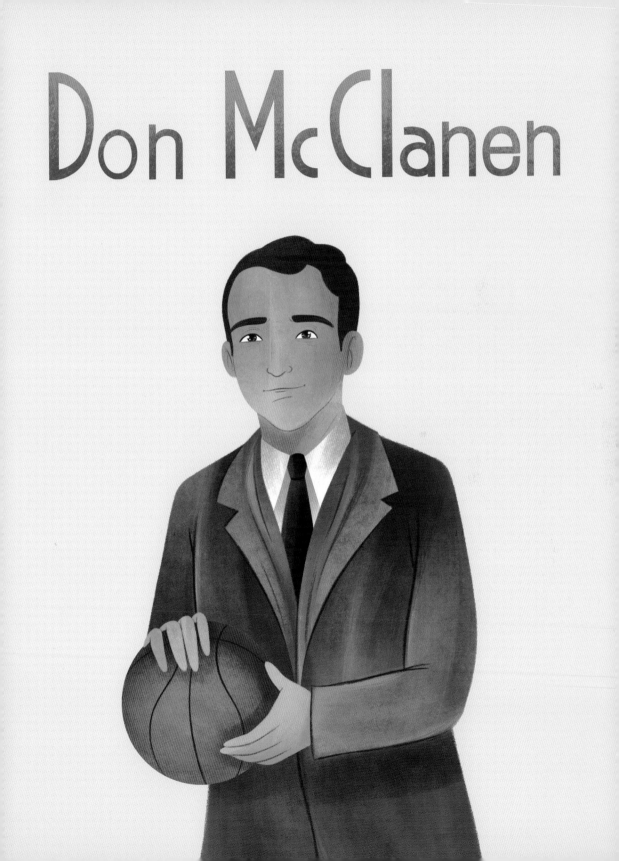

Dietrich Bonhoeffer
Anti-Nazi Maverick

{ 1906–1945 }

Dietrich Bonhoeffer was born into a talented and intelligent German family. His father, Karl, was the most famous psychiatrist in Germany. His mother homeschooled Dietrich and her other seven children—all of whom were musically and intellectually gifted. After earning his doctorate in theology at the University of Berlin, Dietrich became an ordained Lutheran pastor. He traveled to New York City to continue his studies at Union Theological Seminary. Dietrich often attended services at the African Methodist Episcopal Church, where he grew to appreciate African-American spirituals. He enjoyed collecting recordings of these songs.

In 1931, Dietrich returned to Germany. In his book *Life Together*, he states, "Jesus Christ lived in the midst of his enemies. So the Christian, too, belongs not in the seclusion of a cloistered life but in the thick of foes."[11] A strong opponent of Nazism, Dietrich became the leader of a secret seminary. When Nazis shut it down in 1937, the Gestapo banned Bonhoeffer from teaching and preaching.

Bonhoeffer resisted. He became a leader in the Confessing Church—a Christian group opposed to Nazi policies. After much prayer and soul searching, Bonhoeffer joined high-ranking military officers in the Abwehr, a German intelligence organization, plotting to kill Adolf Hitler.

Following his engagement to Maria von Wedemeyer, Bonhoeffer was arrested when money used to help Jews escape to Switzerland was traced back to him. Charged with conspiracy, he was imprisoned and later hanged in April 1945—just weeks before Hitler killed himself. Bonhoeffer's book *The Cost of Discipleship* remains a theological classic.

DIETRICH BONHOEFFER

Frederick Douglass

Abolitionist Statesman

{ 1818–1895 }

Born a slave on a Maryland plantation, Frederick Douglass had several cruel masters. He was a teenager when a white Methodist minister told him about Jesus. Frederick believed. "I saw the world in a new light and my great concern was to have everybody converted...and especially did I want a thorough acquaintance with the contents of the Bible."[12]

His master's wife taught Frederick the alphabet even though that was against the law. He learned to read newspapers and the Bible. He longed to be free, so he disguised himself as a sailor and escaped. In New York, he took the last name Douglass. He married and had five children.

A powerful orator, Douglass became a popular speaker for the antislavery movement. He wrote a bestseller, *Narrative of the Life of Frederick Douglass*. As an ordained minister with the African Methodist Episcopal (AME) church, Douglass spoke out against congregations that supported slavery.

With fame came the danger of being captured, so Douglass fled to England. Supporters raised money to buy his freedom. Returning to New York a free man, Douglass started a newspaper. He met with President Abraham Lincoln to organize regiments of black soldiers during the Civil War. When the Douglass home burned down, many suspected arson. Having lost everything he owned, Douglass moved his family to Washington, DC. President James Garfield offered him an administrative job. President Benjamin Harrison later appointed Douglass as the US ambassador to Haiti. Today his legacy lives on at the Frederick Douglass National Historic Site in Washington, DC.

Hudson Taylor

Seeker of Souls

{ 1832–1905 }

When five-year-old Hudson Taylor boasted that he would grow up to be a missionary to China, his parents never guessed he would forever change the way mission work would be conducted.

Hudson was born in England, where his father was a pharmacist and Methodist lay preacher. Despite his Christian upbringing, Hudson became a rebellious teenager. He had a conversion experience at age seventeen when he read a gospel tract explaining Jesus's sacrifice on the cross. From that moment, he prepared diligently to serve on the mission field.

In 1854, at age 21, Hudson sailed for Shanghai, China. He found the city war torn and disease ridden. Other missionaries disrespected him because he was neither educated nor ordained. He shocked them by donning Chinese clothing and wearing a pigtail. He moved away from the Westerners to live with the locals. He soon earned their trust. When Chinese looters burned his mission station, Hudson refused to allow the British military to quell the uprising.

Hudson launched the China Inland Mission in 1865. With a knack for organization and a magnetic personality, Hudson's work yielded remarkable results. He established twenty mission stations with more than 800 missionaries and 125,000 Christian converts.

But Hudson's life was not easy. He endured illness, harsh criticism, and financial hardship. He outlived two beloved wives and buried four of his eight children. When Hudson died, the China Inland Mission was the largest Protestant missionary organization in the world. He is buried in China—the land he loved.

Hudson Taylor

Edward Jenner
Father of Immunology

{ 1749–1823 }

Dairy farmers seldom caught smallpox. Why? Did it have something to do with their exposure to the mild cowpox virus? Edward Jenner pondered the riddle for years.

Born in England, Edward was the eighth child of Reverend Stephen Jenner and his wife, Sarah. Friendly and docile, Edward began a nine-year apprenticeship with a surgeon at age fourteen. While visiting farms, Edward noted the workers' smooth complexions. They did not bear the usual pits and scars left by smallpox, a deadly and contagious disease. One in three smallpox patients died—most of them children. During the 1778 epidemic, Jenner spent long days riding from one patient's home to another, contemplating the puzzling dairy workers.

Jenner married Catherine Kingscote in 1788 and started a Sunday school for children in their home. In 1796, Jenner tested a hypothesis. He scraped pus from cowpox blisters on the hands of a milkmaid and inserted it into the arm of his gardener's eight-year-old son. Later, when Jenner injected the boy with smallpox, the child developed no signs of infection. Jenner tested this thoroughly before publishing the results of his vaccination—a term derived from the Latin word for "cow."

Although some opposed vaccination, fearing they might develop cowlike traits, it soon won acceptance. By 1802, Jenner was a national hero. His idea continued inspiring other medical successes more than a century after his death. In 1980, the World Health Assembly officially declared smallpox eradicated. Some estimate that Jenner's success saved more human lives than any discovery in history.

Edward Jenner

Nabeel Qureshi

Truthseeker

{ 1983–2017 }

Born to Pakistani parents who had immigrated to the United States, Nabeel Qureshi grew up in a loving, close-knit family. Raised as a devout Muslim, Nabeel understood Urdu, Arabic, and English by age four. He could read the Quran in Arabic at age five.

His father taught him to vigorously defend his Muslim faith, which he did through high school. In college, he met a Christian named David Wood, who challenged him, through logic and reason, to consider the Bible as God's truth and accept Jesus as his Savior. The two became friends despite their religious differences.

For three years, Nabeel compared the teachings of Muhammad with those of Jesus. He wrestled over what was true and what was not. In keeping with the Muslim tradition, he asked God to show him the truth in a dream. The Lord gave him three dreams. Nabeel found peace in the Bible and accepted Christ, although his parents expressed their disappointment in his conversion.

Nabeel finished medical school and later earned degrees in Christian apologetics and religion. His book *Seeking Allah, Finding Jesus* made the *New York Times* bestseller list. Nabeel became a popular speaker with Ravi Zacharias International Ministries, addressing audiences around the globe. He shared his testimony, explaining that Muslims and Christians do not worship the same God.

Nabeel died from stomach cancer when he was thirty-four, leaving behind a wife and young daughter. His legacy of faith lives on.

NABEEL QURESHI

Sir Isaac Newton

Gallant Genius

{ 1642–1727 }

Tiny and frail, born prematurely, Isaac Newton was not expected to survive, let alone become one of the most influential scientists who ever lived.

Isaac's parents were simple British farmers, and his father died before he was born. Isaac was an avid reader, interested in mechanical gadgets. He liked kites and blew bubbles to watch their colors in the sunlight.

At nineteen, Isaac entered Cambridge University. His professors quickly recognized his genius. At twenty-six, Isaac became head of the math department. He invented calculus, made discoveries about gravitation, developed a reflecting telescope, and explained the motion of planets, the moon, and tides.

Although noted for scientific achievements, Isaac spent more time studying theology than science, writing 1.3 million words on Bible topics. He saw no conflict between science and faith, proclaiming, "The true God is a living, intelligent, and powerful being. He governs all things and knows all things that are or can be done."[13] He attended Anglican services, donated money to buy Bibles for the poor, and helped support new congregations in London.

In 1703, Isaac became president of the Royal Society, a fellowship of scientists that still exists today. Queen Anne knighted him in 1705. Incredibly popular, Sir Isaac remained humble. He never married. His death was regarded as a national loss. His pallbearers included three earls, two dukes, and the lord chancellor of England.

Newton's discoveries are still relevant today—his physics took the Apollo mission astronauts to the moon.

Sir Isaac Newton

Jim Irwin

Moon Walker

{ 1930–1991 }

The son of a Pittsburgh plumber, Jim Irwin fell in love with model airplanes at an early age. His mother hoped he would become a Baptist preacher, but after taking a ride in a barnstorming airplane, all Jim could think about was flying. After high school, Jim entered the US Naval Academy, graduating in 1951. Still longing to be a pilot, he joined the Air Force and flew P-51 fighter planes. He helped design missiles and became a flight instructor. He married and had five children.

Jim signed up for the astronaut corps but was turned down twice. Then one of his student pilots crashed their plane, leaving Jim seriously injured. When he recovered, NASA finally accepted Jim into the astronaut program. In July 1971, the Apollo 15 launch and three-day mission went smoothly. Irwin became the eighth man to walk on the moon. He and astronaut David Scott used a moon buggy to explore the lunar surface for the first time.

Jim's experience in space had a profound influence on his spiritual life. He felt God's presence more than ever before. He said, "I feel the Lord sent me to the moon so I could return to earth and share his Son, Jesus Christ."[14]

When Jim retired, he established the High Flight Foundation to encourage others to seek God's destiny for their lives. Jim received many awards before he died from a heart attack. He is buried at Arlington National Cemetery.

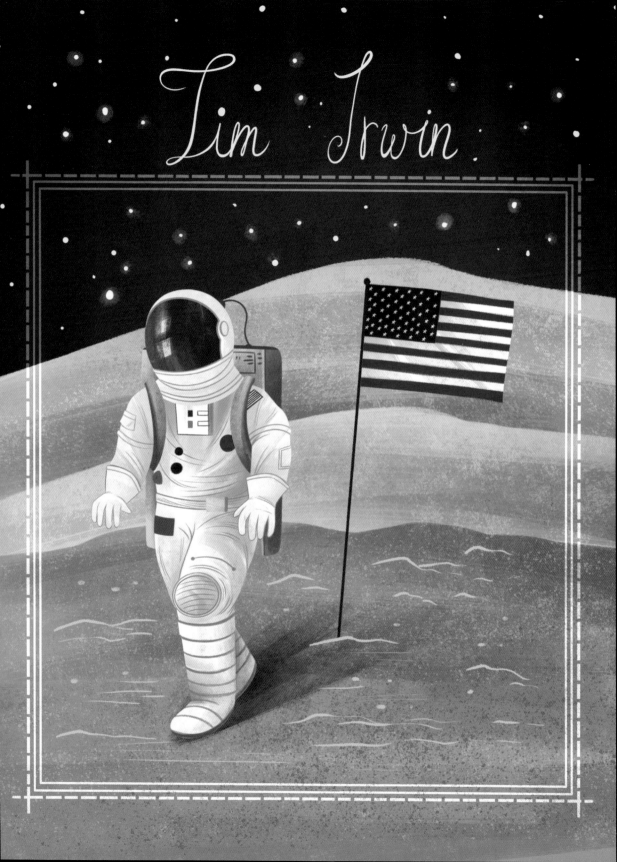

John Harper

Titanic *Hero*

{ 1872–1912 }

John Harper had a passion for preaching. Born to Christian parents in Scotland, John dedicated his life to Christ at age fourteen. At eighteen, he preached in parks and on street corners. His sermons were passionate and powerful. In 1895, the Baptist Pioneer Mission hired him as an evangelist. John's church in Glasgow quickly grew to 900 members.

He married Annie Bell, who died not long after giving birth to a daughter. Harper continued to preach in Scotland and England, earning a reputation as a fervent speaker. In 1910, he preached at the Moody Memorial Church in Chicago. There his vibrant sermons were enthusiastically received, and the congregation asked him to return.

In April 1912, Harper booked passage on the *Lusitania*. Due to a scheduling change, he sailed on the *Titanic* instead. His six-year-old daughter and her aunt traveled with him. When the ship struck an iceberg on that fateful night of April 15, Harper helped his daughter and her aunt into a lifeboat. He did the same for others, taking time to pray with the fearful and reminding them of Christ's salvation. When one man rudely rebuffed him, Harper gave him his own life vest, saying, "You need this more than I do."[15]

Even while struggling in the frigid water, Harper encouraged others to accept the lordship of Jesus. Cold and exhausted, he finally sank beneath the waves. Survivors later recalled how bravely he had faced death, and his parishioners mourned him.

John Harper

Chuck Colson

Bold Prison Reformer

{ 1931–2012 }

Charles Colson was born in Boston, the only child of a prominent lawyer. Bright and motivated, Chuck attended Brown University on a military scholarship, graduating with honors. He served as a Marine Corps officer from 1953 to 1955. He married and had three children, graduating in 1959 from George Washington University Law School.

In 1969, while serving in President Richard Nixon's administration, Colson earned the nickname "White House Hatchet Man" for his willingness to perform distasteful tasks. With the 1972 election approaching, Colson hired an operative to spy on the president's opponents. This and other illegal schemes became known as the Watergate scandal. Colson and several others were arrested. President Nixon resigned.

Before his trial, Colson read C.S. Lewis's book *Mere Christianity* and accepted Christ. He joined a prayer group and shared, "I really was able to see who Jesus is and my need for him."[16] At trial, he pled guilty and was sent to federal prison for seven months. Many doubted the sincerity of his conversion, but Colson never wavered in his faith. He shared Christ with other prisoners, believing God had put him in prison for such a purpose.

Following his release, Colson poured his energies into mobilizing Christians to minister to prisoners. He founded Prison Fellowship Ministries in 1976, an advocacy group for the evangelism of convicts. His autobiography, *Born Again*, became a bestseller.

Besides the prison ministry, his legacy lives on through the Colson Center for Christian Worldview, which equips believers to live out their faith with clarity and courage.

† ChucK CoLson †

Jim Elliot
Missionary Martyr

{ 1927–1956 }

Philip James Elliot was a preacher's kid born in Portland, Oregon. In high school, Jim played football and wrote for the student newspaper. He carried a Bible on campus and spoke passionately about Jesus. Longing for adventure in foreign lands, Jim attended Wheaton College. He took courses to prepare for the mission field and joined the wrestling team to stay physically fit. He wrote in his journal, "I seek not a long life, but a full one, like you, Lord Jesus."[17]

In 1953, he married missionary Elisabeth Howard in Ecuador. Jim heard many hair-raising tales about the fearsome Waorani warriors, who killed intruders with their eight-foot spears. Other natives called them Aucas (or savages). Longing to evangelize them, Jim and four other missionaries launched Operation Auca.

Jim and pilot Nate Saint made several flights over the Auca settlement, lowering a bucket filled with gifts. Using an amplifier, Jim shouted friendly phrases in the tribal language. When the bucket was returned with bananas and a parrot inside, Jim decided it was time to meet the villagers face-to-face. The five men set up camp beside a nearby river. The first contacts were friendly and encouraging. Then unexpectedly, the missionaries were murdered. Jim was twenty-eight years old.

The deaths of the Auca Five shocked the world and sparked a revival of Christian missions. In less than two years, Elisabeth Elliot (Jim's widow) and Rachel Saint (sister of Nate Saint) successfully evangelized the Auca village. All five warriors who murdered the missionaries became Christian leaders of their tribe.

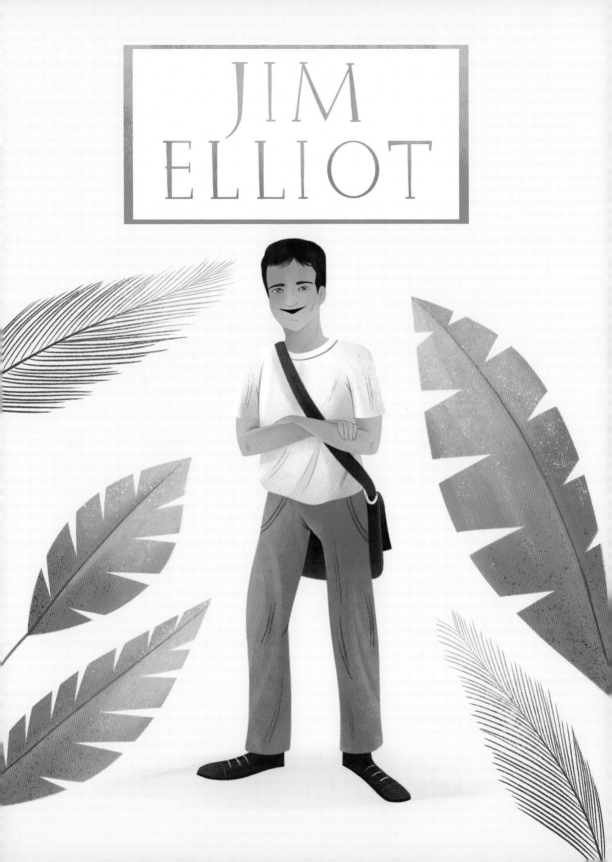

Martin Luther

Reformation Leader

{ 1483–1546 }

For a poor boy like Martin Luther, studying law seemed the best path to comfortable respectability. Luther's father worked hard mining copper to pay for his son's education. School discipline was harsh, and Martin studied hard to avoid punishment. In 1505, Luther earned his master's degree from the University of Erfurt in Germany. He disappointed his parents and surprised his friends by becoming a monk. He was ordained as a Roman Catholic priest in 1507.

While studying the Bible, Luther realized that church reforms were needed. He argued against many common practices, such as selling indulgences (raising money by promising people they would instantly go to heaven when they died). Luther considered this morally wrong and unbiblical. He nailed a list of his criticisms, called the 95 Theses, to the door of the Wittenberg Cathedral in 1517.

Luther's boldness angered church authorities. Declared a heretic, he was excommunicated from the church in 1520. Some officials wanted to kill the troublesome priest, but a friend hid him in a remote castle. Luther caused further outrage by translating the New Testament into German so the average citizen, unable to read Latin or Greek, could understand God's Word.

In 1525, he married a former nun named Katharina von Bora, and the couple had six children. They lived in an empty monastery, which they filled with guests and paying residents. Luther started the first Protestant congregation—the beginning of the Lutheran Church. An enthusiastic music lover, Luther wrote about thirty-six hymns. One of the most famous is "A Mighty Fortress Is Our God."

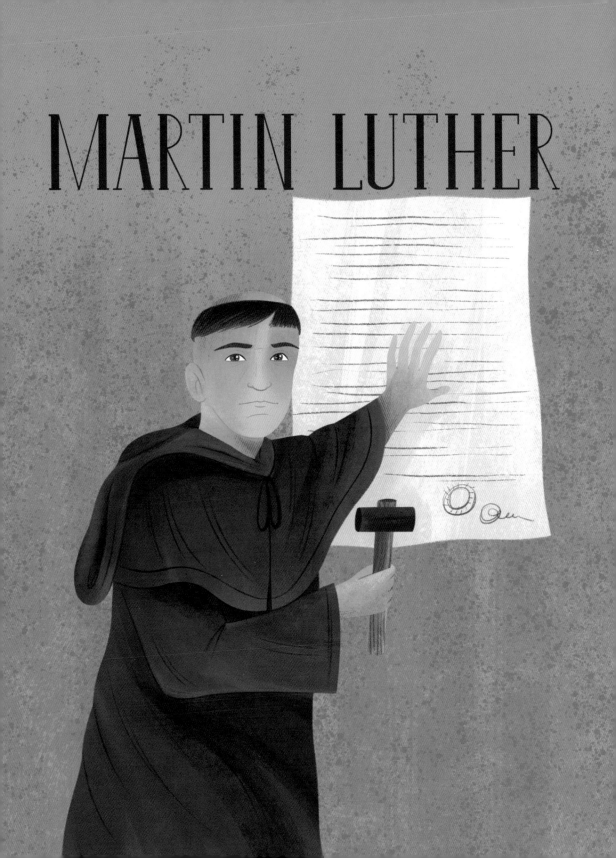

André Trocmé

Fearless Resister

{ 1901–1971 }

A descendent of French Huguenots, André Trocmé was born in France. After earning a theology degree from Saint-Quentin University, he studied religion in Paris and at Union Theological Seminary in New York. He married in 1926, and he and his wife, Magda, had four children.

The year 1940 found André serving as a pastor in the French village of Le Chambon-sur-Lignon. German Nazis took over the government. They ordered French authorities to arrest all Jews. One evening, a frightened Jewish woman came to the Trocmés' home seeking refuge. André and Magda organized an underground network of volunteers to help other Jews. More refugees, many of them children, found their way to Le Chambon. The villagers hid them in shops and farms and helped many escape to Switzerland.

In 1942, the police threatened to arrest anyone aiding the Jews. Pastor Trocmé urged his congregation not to give in to fear: "We shall resist whenever our adversaries demand of us obedience contrary to the orders of the gospel."[18]

The police arrested Trocmé and his assistant pastor. They raided the school and arrested the schoolmaster. The three men refused to sign the loyalty oath to the pro-Nazi government. They spent their imprisonment leading Bible studies for other prisoners. Amazingly, the men were released four weeks later. His spirit undaunted, Trocmé continued to help refugees. After World War II, reports revealed the village had aided 5,000 refugees, more than half of them Jews. No one in the village ever turned a Jew over to authorities.

André Trocmé

Henry Obookiah

Inspired Islander

{ 1792–1818 }

Obookiah was born on the Big Island of Hawaii. He grew up in a small village, where he learned to fish and swim. Warriors from a rival tribe killed his parents, and Obookiah was captured as a slave. At age sixteen, he escaped. While working as a crew member aboard an American merchant ship, he learned English. When he reached New England in 1809, he adopted the name Henry.

One day he sat on the steps of Yale College, weeping because he wanted an education. The president of the college, Timothy Dwight, took the teenager into his home and provided him with tutors.

During this time, Henry accepted Christ as his Savior. Some people in New England felt that natives like Henry could not be converted because they weren't smart enough to understand the Bible. Henry won them over with his charm, intellect, and strong work ethic.

Eventually, Henry became a teacher at the Foreign Mission School in Cornwall, Connecticut, an academy established to give foreign-born converts the skills they needed to become missionaries in their own homelands. Henry also wrote his memoir and created an English-Hawaiian dictionary. He became a popular speaker and a successful fundraiser for the school.

Henry longed to return to Hawaii to preach the good news of Christ. Sadly, he died from typhus in 1818 before he could fulfill his dream. After his death, Henry's memoir became a bestseller. It inspired many Christians to support missionaries in foreign lands, including Hawaii.

HENRY OBOOKIAH

William Booth

Salvation Army Founder

{ 1829–1912 }

William Booth knew what it was like to be poor. Born in Nottingham, England, the son of an uneducated laborer, William became fatherless at age fourteen. He worked for a pawnbroker to help pay family bills. At fifteen, he had a conversion experience so powerful he wrote in his diary, "God shall have all there is of William Booth."[19]

William took the gospel of Jesus Christ into the streets of London. He preached to the poor, the homeless, the hungry. He met Catherine Mumford at a temperance meeting, promoting abstinence from alcohol. The couple married in 1855 and had eight children. Together, they established the Salvation Army in 1878. Volunteers became soldiers of Christ. They wore military style uniforms and formed marching bands. They preached the good news on street corners and in parks. Thieves, gamblers, and drunkards were among their first converts—living testimonies to the power of God.

The organization grew rapidly. The Booths recruited both men and women, believing that they could preach the gospel and serve Christ equally well. But General Booth's ministry was not always popular. Tavern owners attacked the preachers with clubs. Street gangs threw rocks and destroyed their musical instruments. Some clergymen condemned the Booths' unconventional approach to ministry.

The London poor adored William Booth. More than 150,000 viewed his coffin when he died. Thousands attended his funeral, including Queen Mary. Today the red Christmas kettles and volunteer bell ringers are timely reminders that the Salvation Army marches on.

William Booth

Alvin York

Military Hero

{ 1887–1964 }

Life was hard for young Alvin York. His dad owned a meager Tennessee farm and worked long hours as a blacksmith to support his family of eleven children. He taught Alvin how to hunt wild turkeys to put meat on the table. Alvin earned a reputation as a sharpshooter—and as a drunken brawler.

After seeing his best friend killed in a bar fight, York changed. He dedicated his life to Christ. He became a song leader in his church. He hated violence. When drafted to serve in the military during World War I, York hesitated. An Army officer convinced him that being a soldier was not against Bible teachings.

Corporal York distinguished himself in the battle for Argonne Forest in France when his patrol charged a German machine gun nest. York killed twenty enemy soldiers and captured more than one hundred. After returning to the United States, the newly promoted Sergeant York received the Congressional Medal of Honor. Members of Congress gave him a standing ovation. Back in Tennessee, he married and had eight children.

In his diary, published after the war, York wrote: "So I am witness to the fact that God did help me out of that hard battle, for the bushes were shot up all around me, and I never got a scratch."[20] York spent the remainder of his life promoting Christian studies and vocational education in rural Tennessee. His farm is now the Sgt. Alvin C. York State Historic Park.

ALVIN YORK

John Newton
Reformed Slave Trader

{ 1725–1807 }

John Newton's life had many twists and turns. Born in England, John listened to his mother read Bible verses aloud. She prayed her son would become a minister. She soon died, and John became a wild child who was expelled from school twice before he was eleven. His exasperated father, a merchant sea captain, employed him as a cabin boy. Rough, ungodly sailors proved to be bad influences.

One day John was attacked by a press gang and forced to work on a British warship for years. The captain had him flogged. Ashore in Sierra Leone, Africa, John became the servant of a slave trader named Amos Clow, whose African wife treated John cruelly, feeding him scraps and making him sleep on the hard ground. A friend of his father rescued Newton. On the voyage home, Newton read the Bible. When a storm nearly sank the ship, he prayed to be saved, and God answered his prayer.

Back in England, Newton married Mary Catlett and became the captain of a slave ship. As a new Christian, Newton didn't consider slavery wrong. Then God saved him from a second devastating storm. Newton gave up his maritime career to become one of England's most prominent preachers. He actively supported the efforts of William Wilberforce to ban the slave trade. He also wrote hundreds of hymns, including "Amazing Grace," one of the best-loved Christian songs of all time.

His mother's prayer had been answered.

John Newton

Juan Fernando Ortega

Soulful Song Writer

{ 1957–PRESENT }

Juan Fernando Ortega was born in Albuquerque, New Mexico, and lived in the village of Chimayo. His family boasts eight generations of skilled artisans and weavers. As a child, Fernando learned to weave from his uncle. At eight, he learned to play the piano. He frequently traveled with his father, who worked for the US Department of State.

Fernando embraced Christianity in high school when a classmate eagerly shared Bible passages with him. After graduation, Fernando studied classical piano at the University of New Mexico and pursued a music ministry. In 1998, he and his wife, Margee, moved to California, where he worked with Campus Crusade for Christ. He served as music minister at the First Evangelical Free Church in Fullerton, California, under Pastor Chuck Swindoll.

Fernando recorded several albums for various labels before making his major label debut with *This Bright Hour* in 1998, followed by *Home* in 2000, which won the Dove Inspirational Album of the Year award. Steeped in Hispanic tradition, Fernando's music is also influenced by American and Irish folk music, as well as traditional hymns. For Fernando, writing music is a worshipful act. "My records have always been about how the Gospels find expression in a person's everyday life—the sorrowful, the mundane, the joyful."[21]

With three Gospel Music Dove Awards and a Billboard Latin Music Award to his credit, Fernando is a respected musical artist. And although he has little time for weaving, he still owns a large maple, two-harness loom.

William Wilberforce
Bold Abolitionist

{ 1759–1833 }

At fourteen, William Wilberforce wrote a letter to the editor of the local newspaper denouncing slavery. It would become his life's mission.

Born into an affluent British family, William lost his father when he was nine. He went to live with an uncle, who introduced William to powerful preachers, including George Whitefield. In 1776, William entered Cambridge University. He skipped classes, preferring to sit in the gallery at parliament, watching politicians debate social issues. Witty and eloquent, William won his first parliamentary election at twenty-one.

While studying the Bible with a friend, Wilberforce accepted Christ. He wondered if he should become a minister. Pastor John Newton, a former slave trader, urged him to remain in parliament, saying, "It is hoped and believed that the Lord has raised you up for the good of his church and for the good of the nation."[22]

Wilberforce married Barbara Spooner, and the couple had six children. They befriended wealthy evangelicals living in the hamlet of Clapham, near London. After vowing to change the world for Jesus, they collected one million signatures to support antislavery legislation. In 1807, an act of parliament abolished Britain's transatlantic slave trade. Slaves could no longer be bought and sold, but the empire's slaves were not freed.

Wilberforce continued to fight for emancipation. In July 1833, while on his deathbed, he heard the news: Parliament had passed the Emancipation Act, freeing the slaves throughout the empire. Wilberforce died three days later. The 2006 film *Amazing Grace* depicts his forty-six-year struggle and eventual victory.

WILLIAM WILBERFORCE

Richard Wurmbrand

Voice of the Martyrs

{ 1913–2001 }

Imprisoned and tortured for his faith, Richard Wurmbrand survived by God's grace.

Richard was the youngest of four boys born into a Jewish family in Romania. He was exceptionally bright and able to speak nine languages, but he did not believe in God. He worked as a stockbroker and took part in leftist politics. In 1936, he married a Jewish woman named Sabina Oster.

Richard's world turned upside down when he and Sabina accepted Christ in 1938 through the influence of a German carpenter named Christian Wolfkes. Ordained as a Lutheran pastor, Richard preached in bomb shelters and helped rescue Jewish children during World War II. His in-laws died in a Nazi concentration camp, and Richard and Sabina were arrested.

In 1945, when Romanian Communists seized power, one million Russian soldiers marched into his country. Richard immediately began distributing New Testaments to the troops. Again imprisoned and brutally tortured, he asked, "Did I believe in God? Now the test had come. I was alone…God offered me only suffering—would I continue to love Him?"[23]

Christians from Norway secured Richard's freedom for $10,000. He wrote bestselling books about his years in prison. In America, Richard revealed his scars when testifying before the US Senate about the inhumane treatment of prisoners in Communist countries. When the Wurmbrands visited Romania after the Communist regime collapsed, Richard discovered copies of his books in the prison where he'd been tortured.

The couple founded the Voice of the Martyrs, an organization assisting persecuted Christians in more than sixty countries.

· Richard Wurmbrand ·

George Müller

The Orphan's Champion

{ 1805–1898 }

George Müller was a liar and a cheat who was jailed for fraud when he was sixteen years old. His father paid his fines and then sent him to Bible college to reform. One evening, George attended a home Bible study with a fellow student. His life changed when he made a commitment to Christ.

Müller left his home in Prussia to evangelize Jews in England. There he became a leader in the Plymouth Brethren movement. He married and moved to Bristol. Müller soon noticed many homeless kids, and he prayed about opening an orphanage. He shared his plans with other Christians but never asked for funds. Instead, he asked God to provide the necessities—and God did. Müller became known as a prayer warrior.

Over the years, the Müllers and their staff cared for thousands of orphans in several orphanages. The children were educated, well fed, and properly dressed. At Christmas, the Müllers provided presents and sweets and decorated Christmas trees. Charles Dickens, the author of *Oliver Twist*, toured the orphan homes and wrote a newspaper article praising them.

When his wife, Mary, died, Müller yielded his responsibilities to his daughter Lydia and her husband, James Wright. Müller remarried. With his new wife, Susannah, he began a missionary journey that lasted seventeen years. He preached in more than forty countries, including the United States and Japan. When he died at age ninety-two, the city of Bristol came to a standstill as residents took to the streets to watch his funeral procession pass by.

George Müller

Tony Dungy

Football Hall of Fame Hero

{ 1955–PRESENT }

Anthony Dungy was born in the small town of Jackson, Michigan. His parents—both educators—encouraged Tony to exercise his brain and develop his Christian moral character. At fourteen, Tony was elected student body president. He excelled in basketball, track, and football.

He won a football scholarship from the University of Minnesota, where he received the Big Ten Medal of Honor. After college, he was signed as a free agent by the National Football League's (NFL) Pittsburgh Steelers. During his rookie year, Tony became close with teammate Donnie Shell, who dramatically influenced his life by urging him to succeed without compromising his Christian faith. Tony led the team in interceptions his second year—the same year the Steelers won Super Bowl XIII.

After three NFL seasons, twenty-five-year-old Tony became an assistant coach for the Steelers, the youngest assistant coach in NFL history. He married Lauren Harris in 1982, and the couple has three biological children and seven adopted children. Considered one of the brightest minds in the NFL, Tony became head coach for the struggling Tampa Bay Buccaneers in 1996, leading the team to newfound victory and respectability. Next came a coaching position with the Indianapolis Colts and the prestige of becoming the first African American head coach to win a Super Bowl when his team defeated the Chicago Bears in 2007.

After thirteen years as an NFL head coach, Tony retired. He was inducted into the Pro Football Hall of Fame in 2016 and is proud of the open Bible placed on the top shelf of his display locker. "I couldn't tell the story of my career without including the impact Christ had on my coaching,"[24] he said.

TONY DUNGY

G.K. Chesterton

Defender of the Faith

{ 1874–1936 }

Born and raised in London, Gilbert Keith Chesterton was such a slow learner that his concerned parents took him to see a brain specialist. Gilbert loved fairy tales and puppet shows. He enjoyed sketching and enrolled in the Slade School of Art to become an illustrator.

In 1900, he was asked to write articles about art criticism. He eventually became one of the most prolific authors in history, penning 80 books, 4000 essays, hundreds of poems, and 200 short stories, including the Father Brown mysteries. Chesterton wore a flowing cape, and his cane concealed a sword. He stood well over six feet tall and weighed more than 300 pounds. When he got stuck in the back seat of a small car, Chesterton put the dismayed chauffeur at ease by joking about the embarrassing situation.

He married Frances Blogg in 1901. Persuaded by her faith, Chesterton embraced his own in 1922. He used his wit to promote following Christ. He wrote, "The Christian ideal has not been tried and found wanting; it has been found difficult and left untried."[25]

Chesterton loved to debate. His humorous approach won over his audiences and opponents. Those who mistook him for an overweight dunce quickly learned he was nothing of the sort. Several notable authors were strongly influenced by Chesterton's well-crafted verbal gems, including C.S. Lewis, George Orwell, and T.S. Eliot. Politicians Mahatma Ghandi and Michael Collins credited Chesterton with their determination to fight for independence from British rule for India and Ireland, respectively.

G. K. Chesterton

Todd Beamer

9/11 Hero

{ 1968–2001 }

Todd Morgan Beamer never considered himself heroic.

Raised in a strong Christian family, Todd attended Christian schools, excelling at baseball and basketball. At Wheaton College, he studied business and became captain of the basketball team in his senior year, graduating in 1991. There he met Lisa Brosious. They married and had three children. They served as church youth sponsors, and Todd taught a high school Sunday school class. In 2000, the Beamers moved to New Jersey, where Todd worked as an account manager for a software company.

On September 11, 2001, he boarded United Flight 93 for a business trip. Shortly after takeoff, terrorists hijacked the plane. When anxious passengers made cell phone calls to relatives, they learned about the attacks on the World Trade Center in New York and the Pentagon in Washington, DC. Authorities believed the Flight 93 hijackers intended to crash into the White House or the US Capitol building.

Todd spoke with the GTE Airfone operator, explaining that some passengers would attempt to retake control of the plane. After reciting the Lord's Prayer and Psalm 23 with the operator, Todd asked her to call his family and tell them how much he loved them. His last known words were, "Are you guys ready? Let's roll."[26]

The hijakers' plan was thwarted, but sadly, the passengers' brave attempt to regain control of the plane did not succeed. It crashed in a Pennsylvania field, killing everyone on board. Memorials, schools, and even a post office have been dedicated to Todd Beamer—a man of extraordinary faith and courage.

todd Beamer

James A. Garfield

Preacher President

{ 1831–1881 }

On March 4, 1881, James Abram Garfield became the twentieth president of the United States.

The last president to be born in a log cabin, James was raised by his widowed mother and grew up on a farm in Ohio, never dreaming of becoming president. He wanted to be a seaman. But he was baptized at eighteen, eventually became a lay minister, and preached his first sermon at twenty-two. James compared the military career of Napoleon to the true conqueror, Jesus. He urged his spellbound congregation to follow Christ, who is "full of love and compassion, who will stand by you in life and death and eternity."[27]

After graduating from college in 1856, Garfield became a teacher. He amazed students by writing with both hands at the same time in different languages—Latin and Greek. He married Lucretia Rudolph in 1858, and the couple had seven children.

At age twenty-eight, Garfield was elected to the Ohio legislature. He studied law, passing the bar in 1860. During the Civil War, he rose to the rank of major general in the Union Army. He later served nine terms in Congress. Garfield reluctantly accepted the presidential nomination at the 1880 Republican convention and won the presidential election. At his inauguration, he gave an impassioned plea for civil rights for former slaves. He hired four African Americans for his administration.

Shot by a disgruntled supporter, Garfield served only six months and fifteen days. His statue stands on the US Capitol grounds, commemorating his brief but shining presidency.

John M. Perkins
Civil Rights Activist

{ 1930–PRESENT }

The son of a Mississippi sharecropper, John Perkins grew up in extreme poverty. His mother died from malnutrition before his first birthday. John endured oppressive racism. White boys shot at him with BB guns. He dropped out of school in third grade. When John was seventeen, his older brother, a World War II veteran, was murdered by a town marshal. John fled to California and vowed never to return to Mississippi.

John worked as a janitor and a welder. He married Vera Mae Buckley in 1951, and the couple had four children. Their son Spencer took John to a Bible class. "In that Sunday school, I finally met Jesus," John said. "Almost immediately God began to do something radical in my heart. He began to challenge... my hatred toward others...If I had not met Jesus, I would have died carrying that heavy burden of hate to my grave."[28]

In 1960, Perkins returned to Mississippi to establish the Voice of Calvary Ministries. A bold spokesperson for civil rights, he endured harassment, beatings, and imprisonment. Perkins returned to California in 1982 to establish the Harambee Ministries in northern Pasadena, a community with a high crime rate. He started Good News Bible Clubs, technology centers, and internship programs.

The author of several inspiring books, Perkins has received fourteen honorary degrees from colleges across the country. The John and Vera Mae Perkins Foundation spreads the gospel of Jesus Christ to transform lives and reconcile communities.

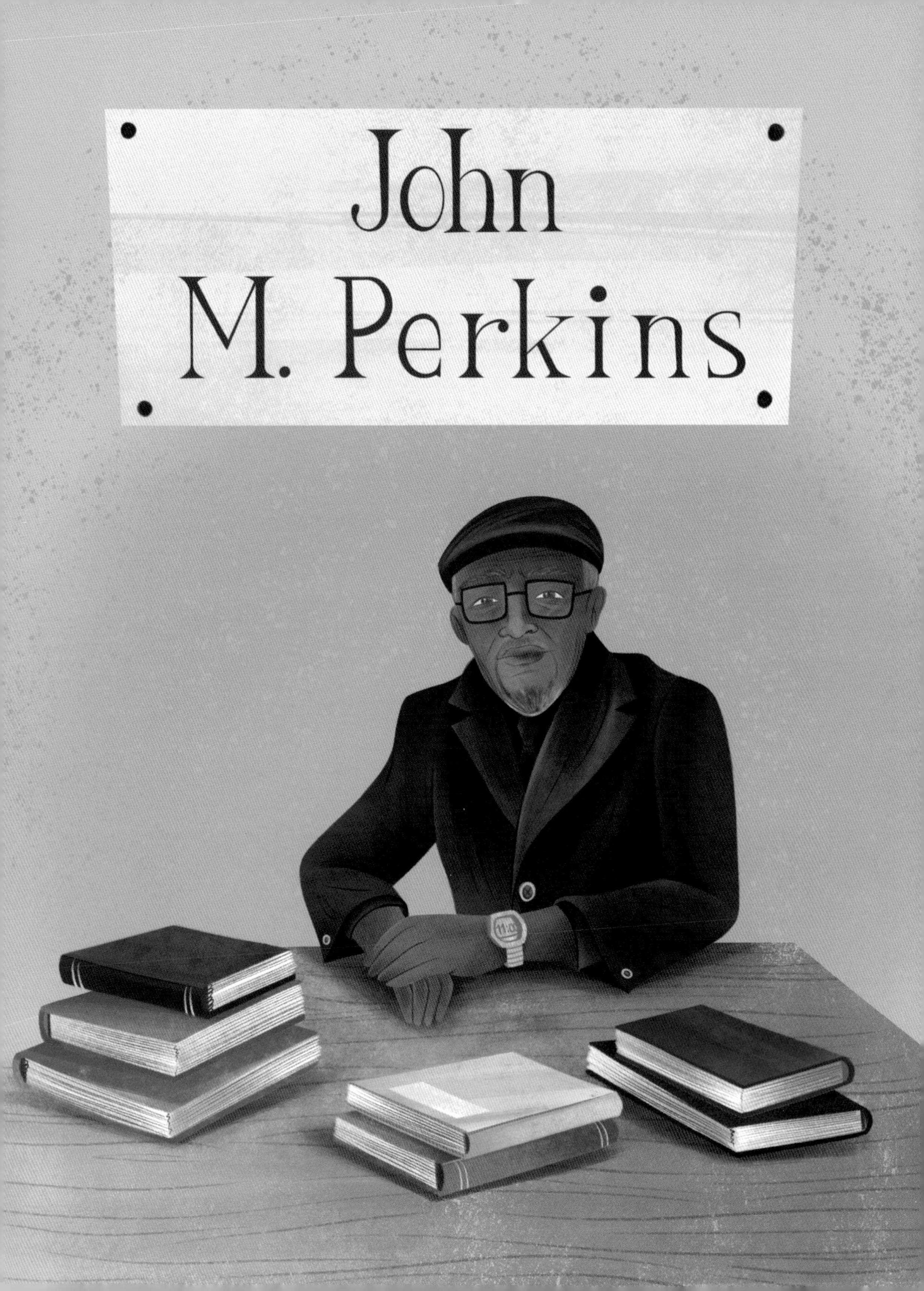
John
M. Perkins

Saint Francis of Assisi
Patron Saint of Italy

{ 1181–1266 }

Giovanni Francesco di Pietro di Bernardone grew up rich and spoiled. He enjoyed archery and horseback riding...and wild parties. His father, a wealthy cloth merchant, indulged him. Francis longed to be a knight, so when the city of Assisi declared war on the province of Perugia, Francis joined the militia. Captured in battle and imprisoned, Francis became ill during his yearlong captivity. When his father paid his ransom, Francis was released.

He returned home a changed man. Francis believed God wanted him to serve the poor and reform the church. He gave away his belongings. When he gave away family funds, his outraged father pressed charges against him in court.

Francis and several friends went away to live in the mountains. They took care of lepers and homeless people. When some robbers stole from them, Francis sent food to their hideout. Moved by this gesture, the robbers gave up crime and joined Francis's community to serve the poor. They eventually became known as the Franciscans.

In 1219, Francis accompanied Christian armies to Egypt during the Fifth Crusade. He daringly crossed enemy lines to preach the gospel to Sultan al-Malik al-Kamil. The sultan remained unconverted, but he was impressed by Francis's boldness.

Known for his kindness to animals, Francis was also a powerful preacher who spoke bluntly about sin and the need to repent. Some criticized Francis for being foolish or delusional. Others believe he followed Jesus's example in his everyday life. Today, the Franciscans are the largest order in the Roman Catholic Church.

Saint Francis

Zhang Boli

Chinese Evangelist

{ 1959–PRESENT }

Zhang Boli will never forget June 4, 1989. On that day, twenty-nine-year-old Zhang became a fugitive. The two-week pro-democracy demonstration at Tiananmen Square in Beijing came to a brutal conclusion when the Chinese Communist government sent tanks and troops armed with assault rifles to disperse the protesters. As students tried to prevent them from occupying the square, the soldiers attacked. Hundreds were massacred, and thousands more were wounded.

As the organizer of the Hunger Strike Brigade, Zhang made the government's list of most wanted criminals. He fled the city and spent two years evading arrest. In the far north of China, near the border with the Soviet Union, he met an elderly Christian woman who hid him. She boldly testified about salvation in Jesus Christ and urged him to read her copy of the Gospel of John.

Zhang began to read and couldn't stop. The crucifixion of Jesus moved him to tears. One dark, snowy night, Zhang escaped over the border. Kneeling in the snow, he said, "Lord, if you let me live through today, I will be forever at your service."[29]

Zhang eventually made his way to the United States. Following a battle with life-threatening kidney cancer, Zhang studied theology and became a pastor near Washington, DC. He is married with two children. Now residing in California, he is the pastor of a global network of churches, preaching the gospel of Jesus Christ online to tens of thousands of Chinese-speaking people.

George Washington

Father of Our Country

{ 1732–1799 }

At the age of twenty, surveyor George Washington joined the Virginia militia to fight in the French and Indian War. There were no chaplains, so Washington often led worship services. He chastised other soldiers who used the Lord's name irreverently. In battle, several horses were shot out from under him. He narrowly escaped a deadly cannon blast. Washington soon believed God had a special purpose for his life.

In 1759, he married Martha Custis, a widow with two children. A member of the Anglican Church, Washington served as vestryman for two decades. Kind and charitable, he told his estate manager to feed beggars who came to Mount Vernon, his home.

During the American Revolution, Washington served as commander of the colonial troops. He turned untrained volunteers into a successful army. General Robert Porterfield once delivered an urgent message to Washington and found the general on his knees praying. Washington's nephew George Lewis frequently witnessed his uncle kneeling in prayer with an open Bible.

The war lasted eight years. After the British surrendered, Washington resigned. In his resignation speech, he told members of Congress that "'the patronage of heaven' sustained him and the army through the hellish war. His voice breaking with emotion, he commended 'our dearest country to the protection of Almighty God.'"[30]

Refusing to be crowned king of America, Washington became the first president of the United States in 1789, serving two terms. Washington left a will stipulating the emancipation of his slaves and providing perpetual care for those among them who were sick and elderly.

George Washington

Notes

1   Glenn Sunshine, "Christians Who Changed Their World: Chiune Sugihara (1900–1986)," BreakPoint, http://www.breakpoint.org/2013/03/chiune-sugihara-1900-1986.

2   William J. Federer, *George Washington Carver: His Life and Faith in His Own Words* (St. Louis, MO: Amerisearch, 2002), 23.

3   Ruth Tucker, *From Jerusalem to Irian Jaya: A Biographical History of Christian Missions* (Grand Rapids, MI: Zondervan, 1983), 150.

4   Tony Lane, "A Man for All People: Introducing William Tyndale," *Christian History*, vol. 6, no. 4 (1987): 8, https://christianhistoryinstitute.org/store/magazine/4883/christian-history-magazine-16-william-tyndale.

5   "Father Damien," Encyclopedia.com, October 11, 2019, https://www.encyclopedia.com/people/philosophy-and-religion/roman-catholic-and-orthodox-churches-general-biographies/father.

6   Micky Goodman, "The Long View," *Atlanta Journal-Constitution*, June 25, 2017.

7   Dan Graves, *Doctors Who Followed Christ* (Grand Rapids, MI: Kregel, 1999), 214.

8   "Francis Schaeffer Quotes," AZ Quotes, https://www.azquotes.com/author/13063-Francis_Schaeffer.

9   Billy Graham, *Just As I Am: The Autobiography of Billy Graham* (Grand Rapids, MI: HarperOne, 1997), 28.

10 Alex Murashko, "Interview: Jeremy Lin on Embracing 'Linsanity' Spotlight, Where God Wants Him to Be," *Christian Post*, October 2, 2013, https://www.christianpost.com/news/interview-jeremy-lin-on-embracing-linsanity-spotlight-where-god-wants-him-to-be.html.

11 John G. Stackhouse Jr., "Following Jesus in the Dark," Christian History Institute, 2007, https://christianhistoryinstitute.org/magazine/article/following-jesus-in-the-dark.

12 "Former Slave Frederick Douglass," Christianity.com, https://www.christianity.com/church/church-history/timeline/1801-1900/former-slave-frederick-douglass-11630645.html.

13 Charles Hummel, "The Faith Behind the Famous; Isaac Newton," *Christian History*, issue 30 (1991): 38-41.

14 Jerry Bergman, "Colonel James Irwin: Creationist Astronaut," Institute for Creation Research, October 31, 2013, https://www.icr.org/article/7724/.

15 Douglas W. Mize, "As Titanic Sank, He Pleaded, 'Believe in the Lord Jesus!'" Baptist Press, April 13, 2012, http://www.bpnews.net/37601/as-titanic-sank-he-pleaded-believe-in-the-lord-jesus.

16 Chuck Colson, *Born Again* (Grand Rapids, MI: Baker Books, 1977), 150.

17 "20 Powerful Jim Elliot Quotes," Leadership Resources, October 29, 2013, https://www.leadershipresources.org/blog/christian-missionary-jim-elliot-quotes/.

18 Leslie Hammond, "Heroes of the Faith: André Trocmé," Evangelicals for Social Action, May 19, 2015, https://www.evangelicalsforsocialaction.org/heroes-of-the-faith/heroes-of-the-faith-andre-trocme/.

19 "William Booth," *Christianity Today*, https://www.christianitytoday.com/history/people/activists/william-booth.html.

20 E. Michael Rusten and Sharon Rusten, *The One Year Book of Christian History* (Carol Stream, IL: Tyndale, 2003), 540–541.

21 Kim Jones, "Biography of Fernando Ortega, Christian Singer," Learn Religions, April 26, 2019, https://www.learnreligions.com/fernando-ortega-biography-708459.

22 Christopher Hancock, "The 'Shrimp' Who Stopped Slavery" The Christian History Institute, 1997, https://christianhistoryinstitute.org/magazine/article/shrimp-who-stopped-slavery.

23 Richard Wurmbrand, *In God's Underground* (Bartlesville, OK: Living Sacrifice, 2004), 52.

24 Cody Benjamin, "Tony Dungy says Bible is necessary part of his Hall of Fame locker," Sports Spectrum, August 6, 2018, https://sportsspectrum.com/sport/football/2018/08/06/tony-dungy-says-the-bible-is-a-necessary-part-of-his-hall-of-fame-locker.

25 G.K. Chesterton, *What's Wrong with the World*, chapter 5, "The Unfinished Temple," 1900, https://www.gutenberg.org/files/1717/1717-h/1717-h.htm.

26 Jim McKinnon, "The phone line from Flight 93 was still open," *Post-Gazette* (Pittsburgh), September 16, 2001, http://old.post-gazette.com/headlines/20010916phonecallnat3p3.asp.

27 F.M. Green, *Churches of Christ* (Louisville, KY: John P.
    Morton, 1904), p. 414. See http://www
    .therestorationmovement.com/_states/ohio/garfield.htm.

28 Sarah Eekhoff Zylstra, "The Final Call of John Perkins,"
    The Gospel Coalition, April 2, 2018, https://www
    .thegospelcoalition.org/article/final-charge-john-m-perkins.

29 Zhang Boli, *Escape from China: The Long Journey from*

Tiananmen to Freedom (New York, NY: Simon & Schuster,
2002), 129.

30 Justin Taylor, "The Faith of George Washington," The
    Gospel Coalition, February 20, 2017, https://www
    .thegospelcoalition.org/blogs/evangelical-history
    /the-faith-of-george-washington.

About the Author

Shirley Raye Redmond is an award-winning writer and newspaper columnist. Her book *Patriots in Petticoats: Heroines of the American Revolution* was named one of the best children's books of 2004 by the Bank Street College of Education in New York. She is also a part-time instructor for the Institute of Children's Literature, a sought-after workshop speaker, and a member of the Society of Children's Book Writers and Illustrators.

About the Artist

Katya Longhi was born in a small town in southern Italy and studied at the Art Academy in Florence and the Nemo NT Academy of Digital Arts. In her spare time, Katya loves to read fairy tales and collect snow globes. She currently works as a freelance illustrator based in Vercelli and has shown her art in numerous exhibitions throughout Italy.

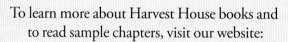

To learn more about Harvest House books and
to read sample chapters, visit our website:

www.harvesthousepublishers.com

HARVEST HOUSE PUBLISHERS
EUGENE. OREGON

TAYLOR · EDWARD JENNER · NABEEL QURESHI · SIR ISAAC NEWTON · JIM IRWIN · JOHN HARPER · CHUCK COLSON JIM ELLIOT · MARTIN LUTHER · ANDRÉ TROCMÉ · HENRY OBOOKIAH · WILLIAM BOOTH · ALVIN YORK · JOHN NEWTON JUAN FERNANDO ORTEGA · WILLIAM WILBERFORCE · RICHARD WURMBRAND GEORGE MÜLLER · TONY DUNGY G.K. CHESTERTON · TODD BEAMER JAMES A. GARFIELD · JOHN M. PERKINS SAINT FRANCIS OF ASSISI · ZHANG BOLI · GEORGE WASHINGTON

ERIC LIDDEL · CHIUNE SUGIHARA
GEORGE WASHINGTON CARVER
DAVID LIVINGSTONE · NICKY CRUZ
TIM TEBOW · NATE SAINT · JESSE
BUSHYHEAD · WILLIAM TYNDALE
RICHARD ALLEN · FATHER DAMIEN
C.S. LEWIS · DIKEMBE MUTOMBO
JEREMY CAMP · ADONIRAM JUDSON
C. EVERETT KOOP · FRANCIS SCHAEFFER
JOHN CADBURY · BILLY GRAHAM
JEREMY LIN · JOHN KNOX · DON
McCLANEN · DIETRICH BONHOEFFER
FREDERICK DOUGLASS · HUDSON